The
Ultimate Camping Guide
And
Camping Tips

2nd Edition

G.A. Iron Cloud

G. A. Iron Cloud

Copyright © 2011-2012

G.A. Iron Cloud

All rights reserved.

ISBN-13: 978-1477466988
ISBN-10: 1477466983

CONTENTS

G. A. Iron Cloud

G. A. Iron Cloud

Introduction
Why We Like To Camp

Camping is now one of the most common ways Americans spend time in the outdoors, and more than one-fourth of the U.S. population camps at one time or another. In fact, it is a growing recreation. In the 1960s there were about 13 million campers. Today there are over 90 million campers.

When you think about it, camping seems like a very strange activity for the modern person.

Although our society is incredibly fond of our creature comforts, we still need a reminder that they are only a part of the grand scheme of things. Camping or living outdoors can help you reconnect to the rhythms of life and the primitive part of your brain that still loves caves.

Camping is a serene, almost Zen-like experience because you are not nearly as distracted when you are camping as when you are home or at work.

Life whirls about us so fast. It can seem like we are being pulled a million directions simultaneously. With activities like camping, you can take a deep breath and find some space to sort out the priorities in your life. We all need what New Agers call "grounding", where we know deep inside where we stand (both literally and metaphorically).

Camping also gives you a sense of self-esteem you might not get anywhere else. You really have no one to rely on but yourself (and your dog, if you are lucky) when you are camping. You are the only one who can supply shelter, fire and other necessities. It's a feeling of independence and yet a connectedness to life, the universe and everything, especially a strong connection to nature.

Studies have shown that the main reasons people go camping are to escape the stresses and strains of work and to escape daily household chores. This same study found that social interaction was a major appeal of camping. Camping activities were almost always social, and a majority of study participants stated that "who they were with" was more important than what they were doing. The study also found that campers spent time in social settings around their campfire, which was often the center of social interaction. One of the people in the study explained, "We gather most of the time at the fire, there's sometimes twenty or thirty of us that are around the campfire. We talk, we sing, we play cards, tell jokes, play some more cards." Another participant called the campfire, "the center of everything . . . that's our energy."

The campfire is so important for a successful camping experience, both from a physical standpoint as well as an emotional experience, I have devoted an entire chapter to campfire building and management.

Chapter 1 Your Checklist

Why You Need A Camping Checklist

Camping in the great outdoors can be lots of fun. I grew up in Montana and my fondest childhood memories are of camping with my family and camping with the Boy Scouts. It was my father who taught me the importance of a camping checklist.

When my family went camping, we were always prepared. My dad had camping down to a science. Never can I remember a problem or a need in the wilderness for which my dad didn't have a solution.

Not everyone is blessed with being able to go camping in the wilderness of Montana. Camping in reserves and campgrounds can easily satisfy many people who love to go out and just spend the night outdoors. Every good camper need to have a camping checklist in which to see which things are needed and which can be omitted.

Not all things in the camping checklist need to be brought along. A camping checklist is like a reminder of what you might think is necessary to bring on a camping trip. Actually, the items that you bring along your camping trip are what you deem necessary and will depend on what kind of trip you wish to have and where you wish to go and for how long.

Basics of a Camping Checklist

Unless you plan to sleep in a camping trailer, one of the essentials when camping is a tent and bedding. These are usually the foremost items in a camping checklist. Durable tents and beddings are needed because some areas can become quite cold and the terrain may be bumpy and rough. Along with the tents, you will need a ground mat or sheet to protect yourself from the cold ground and a sleeping bag.

Other essentials you will need to check out in your camping checklist are cooking utensils and supplies. A burner or stove is one of the essentials in camping. Nowadays, making a campfire in any random part of the forests or filed may be dangerous since it may cause an uncontrollable fire. Many camping checklists encourage camping stoves and burners.

Included in the cooking supplies and equipment for a camping checklist are pots and pans, matches, plates, utensils, cups and detergent for washing. It is important to bring detergent for washing the plates etc that you use for eating because sometimes wild animals are attracted by the smell of food. Other things, which should be checked on your camping checklist, are flashlights, batteries, sealed food containers, food, and many others that you might fond necessary.

A camping checklist functions to remind people of the things that might want to bring, Although there are essentials that you really need to bring along, not all the things on the camping checklist are necessary. It all depends on the location and time of year that you intend to go camping. The length of you trip is also a factor to the amount of things you will need to bring along.

Buying Discount Camping Gear On Ebay

Online auction sites like eBay are the biggest and best malls on the planet. Although there are specialized online auction sites for certain things (Bidz for jewelry, for example), perhaps the best online auction site for finding quality discount camping gear is still the originator, eBay, which is one of the safest of online auction sites if you just keep your common sense with you when checking out the eBay auctions.

Which category

EBay auctions are divided into categories for ease of finding what kind of auctions you want. Discount camping gear falls into a few of these categories, including, but not limited to:
- Camping, hiking, backpacking (considered all one category)

- Sporting Goods
- Hunting (even if you don't hunt, you can often find discount camping equipment in this category)
- Canoes, Kayaks Rafts
- Wholesale Lots
- Fishing
- Climbing

Some security tips

Most sellers on eBay are reputable and are eager for repeat business. Because eBay now insists on sellers registering their credit card information with eBay, a lot of scammers fell by the wayside. Still, there's always someone who tries to get away with something. You can usually tell a scam pretty quickly.

Avoid any auctions on discount camping gear or anything else if the auction description is in all capitals, has extremely poor grammar or says this auction is to benefit a good cause which is not a registered charity. If there is a sob story connected with the discount camping gear auction, run. If you email the seller to ask questions and they do not respond or respond without actually answering the question, run. If they ask you to pay by wire, also run.

The big disadvantage of buying discount camping gear on eBay is that you can't physically inspect the item before you bid. But this is not the disadvantage it once was. All reputable eBay sellers will happily outline their return and refund policies before you make a bid.

You can also check a seller's feedback rating to see what kind of reputation the seller has. Keep in mind that a low feedback rating does not always mean a bad seller - it usually means a new seller. You can even email those customers who gave feedback to ask for references. This is considered okay to do, but some people won't respond just because they are too busy, not because they are out to get you.

Here's my personal checklist:

HYGIENE/CLEANING
 - First aid kit
- Trash bags
- Bath/wash/dish cloths
- Soap
- Toilet paper
- Clothes line and pins
- Small broom and dust pan
- Lotion, sunscreen
- Insect repellent, insect candles
- Lip balm
- Toothbrush, toothpaste
- Comb/hair brush, deodorant
- Medications

CLOTHING
- Large bag for dirty clothes

- Long pants
- Shorts
- T-shirts
- Button up long/short sleeve shirt
- Sweater/sweatshirts and pants
- Underwear/long johns/socks
- Sleepwear
- Hiking boots, tennis shoes
- Bathing suit
- Hat
- Sunglasses
- Gloves
- Heavy/rain jacket and pants

MISC
- Hammer for tents stakes
- Extra tent stakes (not wire ones)
- Duct tape
- Bungee cords
- Plastig garbage bags
- Fold up saw
- Hot dog/marshmallow skewers

COOKING/EATING
- Groceries
- Tub for washing dishes
- Ice chests (2 sizes)
- Ice
- Stove, grill, cooking grate
- Steel wool and brush
- Lighter fluid, charcoal
- Matches, lighter

- BBQ utensils
- Hot dog skewers / pie irons
- Tea/coffee kettle
- Coffee/hot chocolate/tea
- 5 gallon water container
- Cups, plates
- Forks, spoons, knives
- Pots/pans/Dutch oven
- Spatula, serving spoons

SHELTER/SLEEPING
- Maps
- Tents/Poles/Stakes/ Tarps (2)/ Ropes
- Ground Pad/air mattress
- Sleeping bag
- Blankets, Pillows
- Chairs
- Lantern/mantles
- Propane bottles
- Flashlights with batteries
- Fishing stuff
- Hand saw, small hatchet, mallet
- Pocket knife / machete
- Shovels
- Fire extinguisher
- Back pack
- Paper/pencil
- Binoculars & field guides
- Camera/film
- Games (board/outdoor games)
- Water bottles

Chapter 2 Campfire

Sitting around a blazing campfire is one of the best things about camping. Roasting marshmallows and hot dogs is a memory unto itself. But make sure you know how to build a fire and how to properly extinguish it.

Ideally, campfires should be made in a fire ring. If a fire ring is not available, a temporary fire site may be constructed. Bare rock or bare ground is ideal for a fire site. Alternatively, turf may be cut away to form a bare area and carefully replaced after the fire has cooled to minimize damage. Another way is to cover the ground with sand, or other soil mostly free of flammable organic material, to a depth of a few inches. A ring of rocks is sometimes constructed around a fire. Fire rings, however, do not fully protect material on the ground from catching fire. Flying embers are still a threat, and the fire ring may become hot enough to ignite material in contact with it.

Safety measures

Avoid building campfires under hanging branches or over steep slopes, and clear a ten-foot diameter circle around the fire of all flammable debris.

11

Have lots of water nearby and a shovel to smother an out-of-control fire with dirt. Dirt will choke a fire fast. Just make sure it is easy for you to get shovelfuls of dirt easily. If the ground is hard, it will be difficult to dig enough dirt fast enough to keep the fire under control or to extinguish it.

Minimize the size of the fire to prevent problems from occurring. The larger the fire, the more potential there is for nearby trees, brush, or grass to catch fire. Keep the fire to a size that's needed.

Never leave a campfire unattended. If you are going to be gone for only a few minutes, then use your own judgment. But if you will be away from your fire for 15

minutes or longer, then either extinguish it, or get someone to watch it for you.

When extinguishing a campfire, use plenty of water, then stir the mixture and add more water. Afterward, check that there is no burning embers left whatsoever. If water is unavailable, use dirt. Take a green leaf and place it on your coals, if the leaf curls up the coals are still too hot.

Never bury hot coals, they can continue to burn and cause root fires or wildfires. Be aware of roots if digging a hole for your fire.

Building the fire

There are a variety of designs to choose from in building a campfire. A functional design is very important in the early stages of a fire. Most of them make no mention of wood - in most designs, wood is never placed on a fire until the kindling is burning strongly.

Tipi Fire

The tipi fire-build takes some patience to construct. First, the tinder is piled up in a compact heap. The smaller kindling is arranged around it, like the poles of a tipi. For added strength, it may be possible to lash some of the sticks together. A tripod lashing is quite difficult to execute with small sticks, so a clove hitch should suffice. (Synthetic rope should be avoided, since it produces pollutants when it burns.) Then the larger kindling is arranged above the smaller kindling, taking care not to collapse the tipi. A separate tipi as a shell around the first one may work better. Tipi fires are excellent for producing heat to keep people warm. However, one downside to a Tipi fire is that when it burns, the logs become unstable and can fall over. This is especially concerning with a large fire.

A lean-to fire-build starts with the same pile of tinder as the tipi fire-build. Then, a long, thick piece of kindling is driven into the ground at an angle, so that it overhangs the tinder pile. The smaller pieces of kindling are leaned against the big stick so that the tinder is enclosed between them.

In an alternative method, a large piece of fuel wood or log can be placed on the ground next to the tinder pile. Then kindling is placed with one end propped up by the larger piece of fuel wood, and the other resting on the ground, so that the kindling is leaning over the tinder pile. This method is useful in very high winds, as the piece of fuel wood acts as a windbreak.

A hybrid style fire

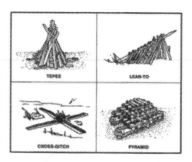

A log cabin fire-build or pyramid fire likewise begins with a tinder pile. The kindling is then stacked around it, as in the construction of a log cabin. The first two kindling sticks are laid parallel to each other, on opposite sides of the tinder pile. The second pair is laid on top of the first, at right angles to it, and also on opposite sides of the tinder. More kindling is added in the same manner. The smallest kindling is placed over the top of the assembly. Of all the fire-builds, the log cabin is the least vulnerable to premature collapse, but it is also inefficient, because it makes the worst use of convection to ignite progressively larger pieces of fuel. However, these qualities make the log cabin an ideal cooking fire as it burns for a long period of time and can support cookware.

A variation on the log cabin starts with two pieces of wood with a pile of tinder between them, and small kindling over the tops of the logs, above the tinder. The tinder is lit, and the kindling is allowed to catch fire. When it is burning briskly, it is broken and pushed down into the consumed tinder, and the larger kindling is placed over the top of the logs. When that is burning well, it is also pushed down. Eventually, a pile of kindling should be burning between two pieces of wood. The logs will eventually catch fire from it.

Another variation is called the funeral pyre method because it is used for building funeral pyres. Its main difference from the standard log cabin is that it starts with thin pieces and moves up to thick pieces. If built on a large scale, this type of fire-build collapses in a controlled manner without restricting the airflow.

Crossfire is another variation in which two pieces of fuel wood are placed parallel on the ground with tinder between them. Once the kindling is going strong, alternating perpendicular layers of wood are placed across the two base pieces. This type of fire is excellent for producing coals for cooking.

A hybrid fire combines the elements of both the tipi and the log cabin creating an easily lit yet stable fire structure. The hybrid is made by first erecting a small tipi and then proceeding to construct a log cabin around it. This fire structure borrows benefits from both fire types: the tipi allows the fire to ignite easily and the log cabin sustains the fire for a long period of time.

Lighting the fire

Once the fire structure is built, the next step is to light the tinder, using either an ignition device such as a match or a lighter. A reasonably skillful fire-builder using reasonably good material will only need one match. The tinder will burn brightly, but be reduced to glowing embers within half a minute. If the kindling does not catch fire, the fire-builder must gather more tinder, determine what went wrong and try to fix it.

One of five problems can prevent a fire from lighting properly: wet wood, wet weather, too little tinder, too much wind, or a lack of oxygen. Rain will, of course, douse a fire, but a combination of wind and fog also has a stifling effect. Metal fire rings generally do a good job of keeping out wind, but some of them are so high as to impede the circulation of oxygen in a small fire. To make matters worse, these tall fire rings also make it very difficult to blow on the fire properly.

Steady, forceful blowing may be in order for a small fire in an enclosed space that has mysteriously slowed down, but blowing may extinguish a fire if it is done abruptly or when it is not needed. Most large fires easily create their own circulation, even in unfavorable conditions, but the variant log-cabin fire-build suffers from a chronic lack of air so long as the initial structure is maintained.

Once the large kindling is burning, all of the kindling should be put on the fire, save for one piece at least a foot long. This piece is useful later to push pieces of wood where they are needed.

Once all of the kindling is burning, larger pieces of wood should be placed on top of it (unless, as in the rakovalkea fire-build, it is already there).

For best results, two or more pieces of wood should be leaned against each other, as in the tipi fire-build.

Extinguishing the fire

As previously mentioned, but worth highlighting again, leaving a fire unattended can be dangerous. Any number of accidents might occur in the absence of people, leading to property damage, personal injury or possibly a wildfire. Ash is a very good insulator, so embers left overnight will only lose a fraction of their heat. It is even possible to restart the new day's fire by using the embers as an igniting device.

Large amounts of water can be very useful for extinguishing a fire. To properly cool a fire, water should be splashed on all the embers, including places that are not glowing red. Splashing the water is both more effective and efficient in extinguishing the fire. The water will boil violently and carry ash in the air with it, dirtying anything nearby but not posing a safety hazard. The water should be poured until the hissing noises stop. Then the ashes should be stirred with a stick to make sure that the water has penetrated all the layers; if the hissing continues, more water should be added. A fire is fully extinguished if the ashes are cool to the touch.

If water is scarce, sand may be used. The sand will deprive the fire of oxygen quite well, but it is much less effective than water at absorbing heat. Once the fire has been covered thoroughly with sand, all water that can be spared should be poured on it, and the sand stirred into the ash.

When winter or "ice" camping with an inch or more of snow on the ground, neither of the above protocols is necessary-simply douse visible flames before leaving.

Finally, in lightly used wilderness areas, it is best to replace anything that was moved while preparing the fire site, and scatter anything that was gathered, so that it looks as natural as possible. Make absolutely certain that anything that was in or near the fire is fully cooled before following this protocol.

G. A. Iron Cloud

Chapter 3 Tents

General tent considerations

Tent fabric may be made of many materials including cotton (canvas), nylon, felt and polyester. Cotton absorbs water, so it can become very heavy when wet, but the associated swelling tends to block any minute holes so that wet cotton is more waterproof than dry cotton. Cotton tents were often treated with paraffin to enhance water resistance. Nylon and polyester are much lighter than cotton and do not absorb much water; with suitable coatings they can be very waterproof, but they tend to deteriorate over time due to a slow chemical breakdown caused by ultraviolet light. The most common treatments to make fabric waterproof are silicone impregnation or polyurethane coating. Since stitching makes tiny holes in a fabric seams are often sealed or taped to block these holes and maintain waterproofness, though in practice a carefully sewn seam can be waterproof.

Rain resistance is measured and expressed as hydrostatic head in millimetres (mm). This indicates the pressure of water needed to penetrate a fabric. Heavy or wind-driven rain has a higher pressure than light rain. Standing on a groundsheet increases the pressure on any water underneath. Fabric with a hydrostatic head rating of 1000 mm or less is best regarded as shower resistant, with 1500 mm being usually suitable for summer camping. Tents for year-round use generally have at least 2000 mm; expedition tents intended for extreme conditions are often rated at 3000 mm. Where quoted, groundsheets may be rated for 5000 mm or more.

Many tent manufacturers indicate capacity by such phrases as "3 berth" or "2 person". These numbers indicate how many people the manufacturer thinks can use the tent, though these numbers do not always allow for any personal belongings, such as luggage, inflatable mattresses, camp beds, cots, etc., nor do they always allow for people who are of above average height.

Checking the quoted sizes of sleeping areas reveals that several manufacturers consider that a width of 150 cm (5 feet) is enough for three people - snug is the operative word. Experience indicates that camping may be more comfortable if the actual number of occupants is one or even two less than the manufacturer's suggestion, though different manufacturers have different standards for space requirement and there is no accepted standard.

If the tent will be used where mosquitoes, gnats and other biting insects are expected, it should have all windows, vents and door openings covered with fine-mesh "no-see-um" netting. Netting will save you a lot of discomfort and will not increase the price of the tent dramatically.

Other buying considerations

Camping season - A tent required only for summer use may be very different from one to be used in the depths of winter. Manufacturers label tents as one-season, two/three-season, three/four season, four seasons, etc.

A one-season tent is generally for summer use only, and may only be capable of coping with light showers. A three-season tent is for spring/summer/autumn and should be capable of withstanding fairly heavy rain, or very light snow. A four-season tent should be suitable for winter camping in all but the most extreme conditions; an expedition tent (for mountain conditions) should be strong enough to cope with heavy snow, strong winds, as well as heavy rain. Some tents are sold, quite cheaply, as festival tents; these may be suitable only for camping in dry weather, and may not even be shower proof.

Size of tent - The number and age of people who will be camping determines how big and what features the sleeping area must have. Obviously, if you have a large family you'll want a much larger tent than a two person outing.

Weather conditions - To allow for inclement weather, some covered living space separate from the sleeping area(s) may be desirable. Alternatively, cyclists on a camping trip may wish for enough covered space to keep their bicycles out of the weather. To allow for sunshine, an awning to provide shade may not go amiss. Some tents have additional poles so that the fabric doorways can be used as awnings.

Internal height - Manufacturers quote the maximum internal height, but the usable internal height may be a little lower, depending on the tent style. Ridge tents have a steeply sloping roof so the whole height is rarely usable. Dome tents slope gently in all directions from the peak enabling nearly the entire height to be usable for a large portion of the tent. Tunnel tents have a good usable height along the centerline. Frame and cabin tents have gently sloping roofs and near vertical walls. To fully evaluate the usable space in a tent, both the maximum wall height and slope must be considered. There are four useful heights used to evaluate appropriate tent height: lie down only, sit, kneel, and stand. The exact heights at which these apply depend on the heights of the campers involved; those over 182 cm (6 ft) are likely to have less choice of tents than those who are somewhat shorter. As a starting point, sitting height is often between 90 and 105 cm (3 ft to 3 ft 6 in), and kneeling height may be between 120 and 150 cm (4 ft to 5 ft). These different heights are useful for evaluating whether certain tasks, such as changing clothes, can be accomplished in the tent.

Number of sleeping areas - Larger tents sometimes are partitioned into separate sleeping areas or rooms. A tent described as viz a viz usually has two separate sleeping areas with a living area in between. If you have a large family opt for the multi-room tent. They are more difficult to erect, but you'll be happier in the long run if you have a few rooms in the tent.

Tent color - In some areas of some countries, there may be restrictions as to what color tents can be, thereby reducing the visual impact of campsites. The best colors for low visibility are green, brown, or tans. An opposing consideration is of safety and calls for visible unnatural colors, such as bright yellow or red. Bright-colored tents can be easily spotted from the air in cases of an emergency. They are important in places where vehicles may not notice a low-visibility tent and run over its unsuspecting occupiers. Campers wandering away from camp will find their way back more easily if their tent is highly visible. Additionally, lost hikers may find rescue by spotting a visible campsite from afar.

Setup difficulty - Some styles of camping and living outdoors entails quick setup of tents. As a general rule, the more robust the tent, the more time and effort needed to set up and dismantle, though specific design attention on quick setup (possibly in exchange for cost and/or weight) can alter that. The style of the tent also has a great impact on its ease of use.

Chapter 4 Tent Care

Keep it dry

You need to keep your tent as dry as possible, no matter what material it's made out of. If you can avoid it, NEVER pack the tent away in its carrier bag while it is still wet.

Any moisture will grow mold and not only make the tent smell bad, the tent will also be subject to rot. When you camp, you shouldn't just have your tent between you and the elements. You need to help the tent out a bit. You need a tarpaulin or some sort of cover - even thick pine branches - that will take some of the brunt of any rainfall.

When the tent gets wet on the outside, such as in heavy rainfall, the inside walls will soon be covered in condensation.

You need to pull everything you don't want to get wet away from the walls. Anything that gets soaked from the condensation will make even more of a wet patch on your tent.

As soon as you can after a rainfall, strip camping tents of everything and dry the bedding, pads, backpacks, or whatever by hanging them on tree branches in the sunlight. The tent needs to be completely empty to dry quickly.

Food in your tent

Never leave food in your camping tents unless you are there immediately eating it. Animals like rats, squirrels, and even bears can smell the food from a great distance and usually will not pass up an easy meal. They will chew holes in your tent to get the food, even if the tent is left wide open. Any food needs to be stored in metal lockers or hung up in trees off of the ground and (mostly) inaccessible to animals. At least, if a squirrel gets your food when it's in a tree, it will not have plowed through your tent.

The greatest danger is bears. Many campers have been mauled or killed because of carelessness with food.

Be like the Japanese and remove your shoes

Unless it's an absolute emergency, NEVER allow shoes or boots inside a tent! The slightest bit of dirt will suddenly multiply beyond belief. Leave your shoes or boots outside under a tent flap, wrapped in plastic bag, or turned upside down on extra tent stakes pounded into the ground within grabbing distance of the tent entrance.

G. A. Iron Cloud

How to make your tent last longer

Most people that own family camping tents which they use constantly each time they go out camping would like their equipment to last for years. Even though camping does cause a lot of wear and tear to the family camping tent, you can take some steps to ensure that they will in fact last longer. First off, you need to exercise greater care in how you handle each of its various pieces and in addition, you must ensure that all the instructions to set up and take down the family camping tents have been followed to the T.

Watch the campfire

You can ensure that your family camping tent lasts longer by taking good care of it in the first place and so you need to ensure that while out camping with the family that you must follow a number of steps that will ensure that you don't end up damaging your tent and which will thus cause it to last longer. So, it means that you should make sure that the mobile cooking stove is never placed close to the family camping tent and even ensure that the tent is placed at a good distance from any campfire.

Use a ground tarp

When you select a location to erect your tent, try to find a clear spot that's not to low - you don't want to

be in the path of drainage in case it rains. Be sure to
Never place your family camping tents close to stumps or over sticks that can cause punctures or tears to the tent, and you should also ensure that the outside is well protected while making absolutely sure not to ever allow the tent to sag.

Buy a tarp that is larger than the footprint of your tent and place it on the ground before erecting your tent. You can purchase a large tarp in Wal-Mart or similar store for less than twenty-five dollars. It will be money well spent. Not only will it act as a moisture barrier between your tent and the ground, it will also protect your tent from small rock punctures as well as keep the tent clean and easier to fold.

Clean immediately

You must also immediately wipe away any stains or spills and use materials to clean off such stains or spillages that are recommended in the tent's manuals, and once your trip in the outdoors is coming to an end, you must store your family camping tents in a proper manner and this may also require you to clean out any dirt or food crumbs left over from your trip which means that the next time you open your family camping tent, it will be clean, and more importantly, you need to ensure that it is dry since otherwise it could be damaged by mildew and other types of fungi.

G. A. Iron Cloud

Use a whisk broom and dust pan

There nothing you can do to really keep your tent floor from getting dirty. People will track in dirt, the wind will carry dust into it, boxes and storage containers will get it dirty when you carry them in and out of the tent.

Buy a dustpan and small broom and keep it handy by the tent entrance. When you see the floor getting dirty, whisk it off. If you do this a few times a day it will make a big difference.

Fold along the dotted line

When breaking camp, people tend to rush and take shortcuts. Make sure the family camping tent is folded neatly and carefully and there should not be any stress to the fabric. The best way to fold a tent is the same way it was folded when you bought it. Pay attention to how it was folded the first time you set it up. Once you find a place to store the family camping tent, you must also ensure that no heavy or sharp objects are placed on top of it, which could cause the tent to rip or tear.

Chapter 5 Camping Knots

Some knowledge of knots is not only very handy to know when camping, they are also useful in everyday life. How many times have you tied something to the top of your car or wrapped a rope around something and wished you knew how to tie the proper knot?

Get a three-foot piece of rope and take thirty minutes to learn these knots. You'll be surprised how many times you use them. Besides, you'll look a lot smarter if you know how to tie these.

Make it fun for the family and get the children involved in the learning process. For some reason, knots fascinate kids. Take turns making the knots, and have a contest to see who can tie a particular knot the fastest. This is a great way to learn these knots.

Clove Hitch

The clove hitch is one of the most widely known and widely used knots. It is a good knot to use when securing something to a post or tree branch, or securing a tent flap.

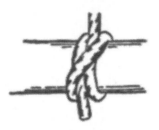

When you use the clove hitch, it puts little strain on the fibers of the rope and less likely to break because it passes around the branch or pole in a single direction. You can see by the illustration that it is also a simple knot and easy to tie and untie.

Bowline

The bowline could be called the Elvis knot, because some people call it the King of Knots. Properly tied, you don't have to worry about the bowline slipping or jamming.

There are literally hundreds of ways you can use this knot. Securing your tent to a tree, making a rescue loop around someone, etc. The knot is not difficult to tie.

Take a few minutes to learn this knot and you'll find yourself using it more often than you can imagine.

Start off by making an overhand loop in the standing part. Then take the free end up through the eye, around the standing part and back where it came from.

Fisherman's Bend

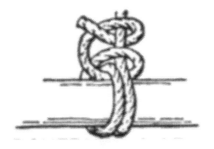

The Fisherman's bend knot is handy for attaching a tent rope to a tree limb or branch. It is simple but strong under strain. One nice thing is it is easy to untie. If it is not under pressure, then it may slip loose.

Fisherman's Eye

The fisherman's eye is also known as the middleman's knot.

If you need to tie a rope through a tarp eyelet then consider this one. It is easy to tie, easy to learn, and easy to remember.

The 2 knots slide together and jam when strained, so it is also a good knot for carrying loads.

Fisherman's Knot

The Fisherman's Knot is one that I use frequently, mainly because I like to fish. It's a great way to tie two fishing lines together. It's also good for joining two small ropes. Tighten each of the two knots separately, and then pull the lines apart to make the knots slip together.

Miller's Knot

Want to close a bag or a sack?

A miller's knot (also sack knot or bag knot) is a binding knot used to secure the opening of a sack or bag. Historically, large sacks often contained grains; thus the association of these knots with the miller's trade. Several knots are known interchangeably by these three names

This is the knot to use. It's a little harder than it looks. Look at the picture carefully, because it can be a bit tricky.

Sailor's Knot

Here's another good knot for securing a rope through a tent eyelet. It's only two half hitches.

Pulling the knot back along the line can make the line tighter.

Unlike many knots, when you want to loosen the knot, it's not difficult.

Sheepshank

One of my favorites. If you have a rope too long that's already tied at both ends, the sheepshank can shorten it for you. I've seen a lot of moving company employees use this knot to secure loads they are hauling. First take up the slack in the rope, and then make an underhand loop and slide it over the blight and pull tight. Do the same to the other end to complete the knot. If you want to make the knot more permanent and more secure, then add another half hitch on each end.

Sheet Bend

If you have two ropes of different sizes, then the best knot to join them together is the Sheet Bend. This is an old sailor's knot that has best tested over the centuries. To tie the ropes together, start with making an eye loop in the largest rope, and then thread the smaller rope through the eye. Tighten the knot before placing any strain on the ropes.

Taut-line Hitch

The taut-line hitch is an adjustable loop knot for use on lines under tension. It is useful when the length of a line will need to be periodically adjusted in order to maintain tension. It is made by tying a rolling hitch around the standing part after passing around an anchor object. Tension is maintained by sliding the hitch to adjust size of the loop, thus changing the effective length of the standing part without retying the knot.

It is typically used for securing tent lines in outdoor activities involving camping, by arborists when climbing trees,[1] for creating adjustable moorings in tidal areas,[2] and to secure loads on vehicles. A versatile knot, the taut-line hitch was even used by astronauts during STS-82, the second Space Shuttle mission to repair the Hubble Space Telescope.

Timber Hitch

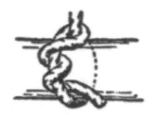

The timber hitch is a knot used to attach a single length of rope to a cylindrical object. Secure while tension is maintained, it is easily untied even after heavy loading.

The timber hitch is an old knot. It is first known to have been mentioned in a nautical source circa 1625 and illustrated in 1762.

If you need to drag a log or a tree branch then use the Timber Hitch, as its name implies. The knot will hold as long as you are pulling with a steady force. When there is slack in the rope, it will loosen.

Two Half Hitches

Here's another useful knot for tying a rope to a pole or tree. This knot is also sometimes referred to as a clove hitch over itself.

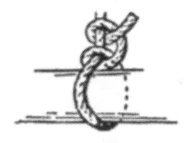

The two half-hitches is a type of knot, specifically a binding knot or hitch knot. It consists of an overhand knot tied around a post, followed by a half-hitch. Equivalently, it consists of a half-turn around a post followed by a clove hitch of the running end around the standing part.

It is a common knot that many people without realizing that it's a real knot with a name. Tighten the knot by pushing the two hitches together then pull on the rope.

Chapter 6 Sleeping Bags

As mentioned earlier, you can get find all kinds, colors and thickness of sleeping bags in places that sell new or discount camping equipment. Some of the best deals are at Army surplus stores. These ex-Army sleeping bags might be all the same color and even have writing on them, but they are often water resistant and warm. Sleeping bags can be used for unexpected overnight guests, for when the mattress is broken or even for kids having a sleepover. Some people even use them as pet beds. And they make great emergency blankets for cars or trucks, just in case you break down on the road.

Basic Sleeping Bag

A basic sleeping bag is simply a square blanket, fitted with a zipper on two or three sides, allowing it to be folded in half and secured in this position.

A sleeping bag of this type is packed by being folded in half or thirds, rolled up, and bound with straps or cords with cord locks. The basic design works well for most camping needs but is inadequate under more demanding circumstances.

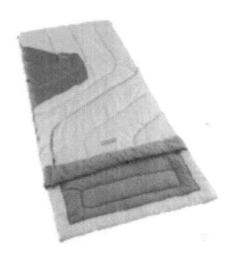

Mummy Sleeping Bag

The second major type of sleeping bag, sometimes called a mummy bag because of its shape, is different in a number of important ways. It tapers from the head end to the foot end, reducing its volume and surface area, and improving its overall heat retention properties.

Some bags are designed specially to accommodate women's body shapes. Most mummy bags do not unzip all the way to the feet. The zipper is a weak point in any sleeping bag's insulating qualities. Together with the tapered shape, this design feature helps protect the feet, which are more vulnerable to heat loss than other parts of the body.

Another design feature is a drawstring, equipped with a cord lock, at the head end to help prevent the escape of warm air. A mummy bag often cannot be rolled like a rectangular bag. Instead, it is simply stuffed into a stuff sack or compression sack.

The bottom of a sleeping bag typically does not provide significant insulation, because body weight crushes the loft of the insulation material. Due to this, it is necessary to use a pad or other less crushable insulation underneath the sleeper, especially in cold weather. Due to this, some sleeping bags do not include insulation on the bottom. Some include a sleeve for holding a sleeping pad. Additionally, some campers, especially ultra light backpackers or hammock campers, have started to use a top quilt, essentially a sleeping bag without a back. Some top quilts include a foot box, while others are just simple blankets.   If you are not camping in very cold weather then this is not a great concern, however if you are camping in a location where the temperatures drop down in the 40s or below, then make sure you have some insulation between you and the ground.

Sleeping bag fillers

Many different insulating materials are available for sleeping bags. Outdoors professionals usually prefer either synthetic fill (e.g. PrimaLoft), or natural fill (e.g. down), and they have debated the merits of these materials for years.

Synthetic fill does not readily absorb water, dries easily, and provides some warmth even when thoroughly soaked. These properties may save the owner's life if, for example, the sleeping bag is accidentally dropped into water on a cold day. Synthetic material is also firm and resilient, so it insulates well even underneath a person's weight. On the flipside, synthetic fill cannot be compressed as much as down and it weighs more, causing such bags to take up more space and weight when not in use. Furthermore synthetic insulation tends to break down faster than its natural counterpart.

Down fill weighs less than synthetic and retains heat better, but usually costs more. Down must be kept dry; a soaked, down sleeping bag may provide even less insulation than no sleeping bag at all, leading to hypothermia. Newer, more technically advanced sleeping bags often have water-resistant shells and can be used in damper conditions. It is also recommended to keep a sleeping bag in a larger sack (storage sack) as opposed to the small traveling sack (compression bag) during long periods of storage. However, many regular backpackers and hikers agree that hanging a sleeping bag, taking care to move the position of the bag on the hanger at intervals so as to not create a "dead spot" (a spot where the fill has been crushed so that it is no longer useful), is the best method of storing a bag for long durations.

Other materials, notably cotton and wool, have also been used for sleeping bags. Wool repels water nicely and also resists compression, but it weighs much more than any alternative. Cotton suffers from high water retention and significant weight, but its low cost makes it an attractive option for uses like stationary camping where these drawbacks are of little consequence.

The Ultimate Camping Guide and Camping TIps

So, there are many uses for camping gear. Don't discount camping equipment for alternatives to everyday problems, or for disaster planning. They are far more useful and practical to be reserved for one camping trip a year.

Chapter 7 Backpacks

Things to look for in backpacks

When you go out camping, you need something in which to carry your essential items that will make your camping trip free of hassles. The proper equipment for this purpose are camping backpacks which offer a number of advantages such as flexibility in space as well as the ability to distribute weight evenly. Backpacks should also be light in weight and durable. I have seen cheap plastic backpacks split at their poorly sewn seams, spilling contents all over the ground.

Standard features

Almost all camping backpacks available on the market today will have standard features such as double compartments and pockets that are meshed and zippered though how much each such backpack can hold will vary from one backpack to the other and the torso range would generally fall between fourteen and twenty-four inches.

Other features to look for in your camping backpacks include hip belt fit, sternum straps as well as compression straps, and some models may even come with removable side pockets and also load stabilizer straps and there are also camping backpacks that are available with and without frames. More on this below.

However, the better option is to opt for camping backpacks that come with frames and here again you can choose between camping backpacks with internal frames or those with external frames. If you choose the more modern internal frames you will get equipment that is more durable and which do not suffer from many of the problems that you will encounter normally with other backpacks since they cleverly amalgamate plastic, foam and also aluminum. Also more details below.

Besides the type of frame or lack of one, you should also look for hip belts, back panels, shoulder straps and overall construction before choosing your camping backpack and of special importance the ability to transfer weight to the hip, and for this the backpack might require use of V-shaped stays and there should also be overall stability of the backpack. Another feature worth noting is to have a hard frame sheet that will provide strength to the backpack and which will prevent sharp objects from poking you in the back.

G. A. Iron Cloud

Next, you should realize the value of the hip belt that is crucial to the backpack since it is this that receives all of the weight of the backpack and so you should look for stiffness that will not allow the backpack to sag beneath its weight, since the softer hip belts are easily worn out and they shift the weight to the hip easily which will tire you out as you walk. The hip belt allows you to rest your back muscles on long hikes.

The great demand for camping backpacks has spawned many online stores from where you can get efficient backpacks that will suit various needs and you can even review different products to get a better idea as to which the most suitable camping backpacks are.

Backpack designs

As mentioned above, backpacks in general fall into one of four categories: frameless, external frame, internal frame, and body pack.

A pack frame, when present, serves to support the pack and distribute the weight of its contents across the body more appropriately, by transferring much of the weight to the hips and legs. Most of the weight is therefore taken off the shoulders, reducing the chance of injury from shoulder strap pressure (many backpacks equipped solely with shoulder straps can affect the posture of a person carrying more than 14 kg (30 lbs)), as well as being less restrictive of the upper body range of motion.

Most backpacks are capable of being closed with either a buckle mechanism, a zipper, or a dry-bag type closure though a few models use a drawstring fitted with a cord lock for the main compartment.

Make sure these compartments are situated so that contents aren't easily spilled out.

Frameless

The simplest backpack design is a bag attached to a set of shoulder straps. Such packs are used for general transportation of goods, and have variable capacity.

The simplest designs consist of one main pocket. This may be combined with webbing or cordage straps, while more sophisticated models add extra pockets, waist straps, chest straps, padded shoulder straps, padded backs, and sometimes-reflective materials for added safety at night.

Because construction is simple and material patterns are simpler, these packs are generally produced inexpensively.

Some outdoors packs, particularly those sold for day hikes, ultra light backpacking and mountaineering are sometimes frameless as well.

External frame packs

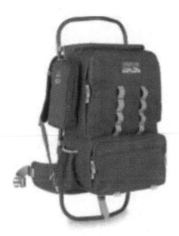

External frame packs were designed carry heavy loads (>20 kg or 40 lb), giving the wearer more support and protection and better weight distribution than a simple, frameless strapped bag. Wooden pack frames were used for centuries around the world. Ötzi the Iceman may have used one in the Copper Age Alpine Italy, though some archaeologists believe the frame found with the body was part of a snowshoe.

Such packs are common in military and mountaineering applications; metal versions first appeared in the mid-20th century. The frame of an external frame pack is typically made from aluminum, other lightweight metal alloy, and recently reinforced synthetic polymers or plastic and is equipped with a system of straps and tautly-stretched netting which prevents contact between the metal frame and user's back.

In addition to comfort, this "stand-off" provides the additional benefit of creating air circulation between the frame and the wearer's back.

For this reason, external frame packs are generally considered to be a "cooler load" than internal frame designs.

External frame packs have a fabric "sack" portion, which is usually smaller than that of internal frame packs, but have exposed frame portions above and below the sack to accommodate attachment of larger items.

In addition, the sack can often be removed entirely, permitting the user to customize the configuration of his load, or to transport a non-conventional load such as a quartered game animal. Military packs are often external frame designs due to their ability to carry loads of different shapes, sizes and weights.

Internal frame packs

The internal frame backpack was invented in 1967 by Greg Lowe, who went on to found Lowe Alpine and Lowepro, companies specializing in backpacks and other forms of carrying bags for various equipment.

An internal-frame pack has a large fabric section around an internal frame composed of strips of aluminum, titanium or plastic, sometimes with additional metal stays to reinforce the frame. A complex series of straps works with the frame to distribute the weight and hold it in place.

The internal frame permits the pack to fit closely to the wearer's back and minimizes shifting of the load, which is desirable when participating in activities that involve upper-body movement such as scrambling over rocky surfaces and skiing.

However, the tight fit reduces ventilation, so these types of packs tend to be sweatier than external frame packs.

The internal construction also allows for a large storage compartment; a few lash points (including webbing loops and straps for sleeping bags and other large items) may be present, but as the frame is completely integrated, it is difficult to securely lash larger and heavier items which do not fit inside the compartment to the outside of the pack.

Internal frame packs originally suffered from smaller load capacity and less comfortable fit during steady walking, but newer models have improved greatly in these respects. In addition, because of their snug fit, the improved internal frame models have largely replaced external frame backpacks for many activities.

G. A. Iron Cloud

Backpacks for outdoor activities

One common special type of backpack (sometimes referred to as a "technical pack" or "frame pack") is designed for backpacking and other outdoors activities.

These types of packs are more complex than most other backpacks. Compared to backpacks used for more day-to-day purposes such as schoolbooks, such packs are designed to carry substantially heavier loads, and as a result most such packs attach not only at the shoulders but at the hips, using a padded hip belt to evenly distribute the weight of the pack to the legs and back for better balance and comfort (this is a must for long hikes and extensive trips through trails.)

The often heavily padded and sometimes semi-rigid shoulder straps are mainly for balancing the weight. They usually (except for those used in ultra light backpacking) have a metal or plastic frame to support and distribute the weight of the pack. Larger packs of this type tend to have a subdivided main compartment.

These trekking packs often have several pockets on the outside; they may also have lash points on the exterior (either directly attached to the frame or webbing loops), so that bulky items may be strapped on, although depending on the pack design and type of trek most backpackers will try to stuff everything into the pack.

Multiday packs typically have a content between 60 and 100 litres (and are about 3 ft /1 metre tall).

Smaller packs with similar features are available for shorter trips.

The most common materials for such packs are canvas and nylon, (polyester), either ripstop fabric for lightweight packs or heavier fabric such as cordura for more typical usage. Most such packs are purpose-designed for the outdoors market; however, it is not uncommon for military surplus packing gear to be sold to outdoors people as well for the same purpose.

City trekkers often favor the cheaper versions of the outdoor packs as they have a large volume and still carry relatively easily.

Outdoors packs, in addition to the distinction between external-frame and internal-frame, can be further subdivided based on the duration of trip a pack might be expected to be used for.

Daypacks hold supplies for a single day's hiking (size about 20-30 litres), while **"weekender"** bags can hold two to three day's worth of gear and supplies (sizes about 40-50 litres).

Larger packs generally have no specific names but are designed to distribute the weight of increased numbers of gear and supplies for longer-duration trips (60-100 litres); such packs often include complex ergonomic support features to simplify the carrying of large amounts of weight.

A third type with little or no frame at all, similar to the book bags used by students and made of light fabric (often nylon ripstop, as mentioned above), is used in ultra light backpacking to eliminate the weight of the frame and heavy fabric used in more typical outdoors packs. Despite their lesser weight, such packs are seldom less expensive than more typical, regular-weight packs.

Chapter 8 Portable Stoves

Different kinds of portable camping stoves

One essential part pf camping is cooking out. Cooking during a camping trip can be very enjoyable and at the same time difficult if you do not have the right tools and equipment. There are two ways of cooking when you are put camping, you can either build a camp fire or cook your food over it or you can bring a portable camping stove and cook with it.

Light weight camping stoves

Some camping stoves are made with a burner and attached to a liquefied petroleum gas container or butane container. They have the same concept as you average home stove except that these are portable and lightweight. The liquefied petroleum gas in it may be limited since the containers vary in size depending on the amount of gas in it. Bring the appropriate size gas container in accordance to the days you go camping.

Camping stoves also need the right size pots and pans to cook your food in. You do not necessarily need to bring too many pots and pans. You just need one pot to consistently boil water in, in case you ran out of bottled water and if you think that river or spring you get water from is not clean. Using the water pot for other foods might taint it with the flavor and smell of the food making the boiled water unappetizing.

When you use a camping stove make sure that you turn it off well. Store the stove outside you tent because if it has a leak, the smell of the liquefied petroleum gas or the butane gas that is sometimes used to light the camping stove might poison you.

Another type of camping stove is the **Trangia** stove. This type of stove has many different models that range from a single burner to a double burner good for many uses. Other camping stoves use methylated spirits to burn or liquid fuel. These need to be handled carefully because they are very easy to catch fire.

The use of camping stoves became prevalent when many people realized the environmental impact of building afire in the forest or field.

The fire scar left on the ground takes a couple of year to recover from the campfire. This made people aware that the environment cannot handle too much campfire burning especially if they are built randomly, just any place the campers wish to build a fire.

Camping stoves help the earth by limiting the exposure of the soil to fires and helping to lessen the environmental impact of open fires to global warming.

Single burner alcohol stoves

The simplest type of stove is an unpressurized single burner design, in which the burner contains the fuel and which once lit burns until it is either extinguished or the fuel is exhausted. There are both liquid- and solid-fuel stoves of this variety.

Because they are extremely small and lightweight, this type of stove tends to be favored by ultra light backpackers as well as those seeking to minimize weight and bulk, particularly for extended backpacking trips. Solid-fuel stoves are also commonly used in emergency kits both because they are compact and the fuel is very stable over time.

The **Trangia** stove is a popular commercial alcohol stove, which is available in many different models, from a single bare burner to an integrated expedition cooking system. Some of these come with a sealing cover, allowing the burner to be packed while still containing fuel, although putting the lid on while the stove is hot can damage it.

An even simpler system is the Sterno heater, in which the can that contains a jellied fuel also serves as the burner. Homemade beverage can stoves (or "Pepsi can stoves") are similar. These are made from discarded aluminum beverage cans, and come in a wide variety of different designs.

Gravity-fed spirit stoves

The traditional "spirit stove" (alcohol or methylated spirits) consists of a small reservoir or fuel tank raised above and to the side of the burner. The fuel tank supplies the methylated spirits under gravity to the burner, where it is vaporized and burned. The gravity-fed spirit stove is still found in many pleasure boats, although it has largely replaced by compressed gas stoves.

Lighting a gravity-fed spirit stove is similar to lighting a traditional Primus stove. Around each burner is a priming pan used to preheat the burner. To light the stove, the burner is first turned on to allow a small amount of fuel to pass through the burner and collect as a liquid in the priming pan.

The burner is then turned off, and the fuel ignited to preheat the burner. When the fuel in the pan is almost all gone, the burner is turned on again, and fuel passes into the burner where it is vaporized and passes through the jets.

These stoves look and even sound a bit like pressurized burner stoves, but the fuel tank is under no pressure. They remain popular for small boats owing to the minimal fire risk they pose in a confined space.

Solid fuel stoves

A solid-fuel stove may consist of no more than a metal plate to hold the fuel, a set of legs to keep it out of contact with the ground, and some supports for the billycan or cooking vessel. This design is scalable, and may be used for anything from tiny backpacking stoves to large portable woodstoves.

More complex stoves may use a double-walled design with a chamber for partial biomass gasification and additional mixing to increase heat output and provides a cleaner, more complete burn.

Among compact commercial models, the Esbit solid fuel stove burns small tablets of hexamine or trioxane in a folding stand made of aluminum or other base metal, and is a German design that dates from World War II. Generally intended for use by a single person, the fumes will tend to taint food if exposed to the burning tablets, and will also leave a messy residue that may be impossible to remove from cookware.

Compact camping and hiking stoves

Smaller, more compact stoves were developed in the early 20th century that used petrol (gasoline), which at that time was similar to so-called white gas and did not have the additives and other constituents contained in modern gasoline.

Similar in design to the kerosene burning Primus-style stove, the smaller white gas stove was also made of brass with the fuel tank at the base and the burner assembly at the top. Unlike the Primus-style stove, however, priming both pressurizes the tank and pre-heats the burner assembly in this type of stove. Once lit, the heat from the burner maintains the pressure in the tank until the flame is extinguished.

The **Svea** 123, introduced in 1955, is among the most popular of these "self pressurizing" stove designs, and is generally considered to be the first compact camping stove.

Optimus of Sweden manufactures a line of similarly designed stoves in which the stove's components are entirely enclosed in a folding metal case, the most popular of which were the Optimus 8R and Optimus 111 (and still in production as the Optimus Hiker).

G. A. Iron Cloud

In the early 1970s, Mountain Safety Research (MSR) designed a pressurized burner stove intended to address performance shortcomings of white gas stoves in cold or adverse conditions, in particular for mountaineering use.

First introduced in 1973 and designated the Model 9 (and later as the XGK Expedition), the MSR stove had four main parts: a free-standing burner assembly with integrated pot supports; the fuel bottle, which doubles as the stove's fuel tank; a pump that screws into the bottle; and a flexible tube or pipeline connecting the pump/bottle assembly to the burner assembly. This type of stove design, with the "outboard" fuel tank held away from the burner, is primed in the same manner as other white gas stoves; however, because the tank is not self-pressurizing, the tank must periodically pumped to maintain pressure to the burner. Most commercial liquid fuel camping stoves on the market today are of this design.

Pressurized burner stoves are now available that are capable of burning multiple fuels or volatile liquids with little or no modification (due to variability in the volatility of different fuels, the "jets" of multi-fuel stoves may need to be changed according to the type of fuel used), including alcohol, gasoline or other motor fuels, kerosene, jet propellant, and many others.

Coiled burner stoves

The "coiled burner" stove is a variant on the pressurized burner design, in which the burner assembly consists of a coiled loop with a small hole in the lower part, through which the vaporized fuel exits and combusts. Generally small, lightweight and cheaply made, these were sold under the brand name "Stesco", "Tay-Kit", "Handy Camper" and others. A more substantial version of the coiled burner stove is the Swiss made Borde stove.

A simple hobo stove is constructed out of a discarded tin can of any size by removing the top of the can, punching a number of holes near the upper edge, and punching corresponding holes in the opposite base. Wood or other fuel is placed in the can and ignited. A pot (or larger tin can) is placed on the top of the can for cooking. Stoves of similar design can be made out of materials other than cans, such as discarded duct pipe.

While simple, solid fuel stoves have several disadvantages. In most cases, only varying the amount of fuel placed on the fire, while fluid fuels may be controlled precisely with valves may control the burn rate. In addition, no solid fuel burns completely. It produces considerable amounts of ash and soot, which soils both the stove and the cooking vessels. In addition, because some of the chemical energy of the fuel remains locked up in the smoke and soot, solid fuel releases less heat, gram for gram.

Multiple burner stoves

Stoves with two or more burners that may be operated together or separately are common for use in base camp, car camping and other situations involving cooking for larger groups. The folding "suitcase" style by Coleman is the best known of this design, and should be used on a flat, stable surface such as a tabletop. This type of stove may have a separate fuel tank for each burner, or more commonly a single tank shared by both burners. Multiple burner stoves generally use compressed gas, alcohol or Naphtha (also known as White gas or Coleman fuel).

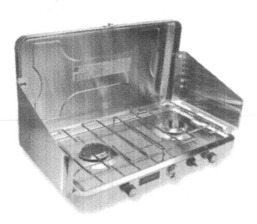

Chapter 9 Campsite Selection

Choosing the wrong place to set up camp has the potential to ruin your camping trip, or at the very least, make it miserable.

One of your main objectives should be not to leave behind any sign that you were there. Try to pick a spot that is obviously an established campsite if possible. We want to leave nature the way we found it, not littered with trash or with crushed vegetation and flowers that have been trampled on. Raw nature is beautiful. Too many times, I seen beautiful scenery scarred by thoughtless campers who had no regard for the ugly footprint of humanity they left behind after breaking camp, a sight that is as ugly as graffiti on a beautiful building.

Here are great tips for picking the right campsite.

1.) Try to select a place provides shelter from the wind. Look for rock outcroppings or natural windbreaks. A special caution for outcroppings: don't camp directly beneath them or build fires large enough to heat the rocks.

A large fire can expand existing cracks or create new ones with the potential for rock to break off and fall on you or your campsite. When we cam on the beach, we park our cars to provide our own windbreak. Inside our "car fortress" we build the campfire and position our chairs for a cozy evening.

2.) Camp on elevated ground if you can. Make sure water will drain away from your tent in the event of rain. Keep in mind that cold air is heavier than warm air. Cold air will flow downhill so an elevated campsite will be warmer.

3.) The same caution applies to camping beneath large trees with dead branches. You may have heard the term "Widow Maker." A large falling branch can be a "Widow Maker" because of lethal results. Also, avoid building fires beneath trees as limbs can catch fire from floating embers. If it rains, trees will drip for a long time after the rain stops.

4.) Concern yourself with protecting streams and creeks. Don't set up camp too close to one, instead stay a few hundred feet away to avoid contaminating them and also to avoid being flooded out by a heavy rain.

5.) Stay away from high weeds and damp grounds unless you love bugs. Make sure that the vegetation around the campsite isn't poison ivy or other such plants. Don't forget, a breezy spot will likely be freer of bugs.

6.) The sun rises in the East and sets in the West. Morning sun is great, but sometimes afternoon sun can be brutally hot and bright, especially in a tent. I always try to orient my tent and choose a site that allows me to bask in morning sun, and have shelter from the evening sun. You might not be able to do that all the time, but if you can, do it.

7.) Animals can be pests if you don't properly store your food. Never store it in your tent. Use a food bag, hoisted in a tree at least ten feet above the ground.

Make sure you camp near a tree that you can use for that purpose and be sure to bring plenty of rope for that purpose. Small animals can be pests, but bears are downright dangerous. It is pretty terrifying to wake up in the middle of the night with a bear in your tent.

8.) Depending on where you are camping, it is wise to check regulations on fires. In the summers, some areas will not allow campfires. Better to call ahead rather to arrive at camp and find out you'll have to eat dry food for the next few days.

G. A. Iron Cloud

Chapter 10 Camping Tips

Camping is lots of fun, but also a lot of work. It's like swimming or horseback riding - you have a great time, but are generally exhausted by it. Camping also means different things for different people. Some call taking a fully loaded RV with home theatre system into the woods "camping". That's not called "camping". That's called "cheating". In order to get the most out of real camping, here are a few tips for less stress and more enjoyment.

Pack light

The most obvious of camping tips is also the one most often ignored. If you are carrying everything you need on your body, then logically you should only carry what you absolutely have to. But I have known many people who want to bring the encyclopedia to read (not an exaggeration), makeup kits and even rock collections. You need to take only what you need - and nothing else.

Your basic needs are bedding, water protection, water carrier, food, any necessary medical supplies, something for fire making and a mobile phone. If you have your dog with you, then you need to carry his or her food, inoculation certificate and water bowl. There are some dogs that don't mind carrying a backpack, but don't over pack it. Everything else is just wants and not needs.

Lower your expectations

One of the other best-ignored camping tips is to not expect much. Don't expect a live-action version of the Discovery Channel on any camping trip. The best camping trips are very low in the drama department. You are there to relax, so just relax. Open your mind to the possibilities, and you will often be pleasantly surprised.

Don't drink the water

Perhaps the most practical of camping tips is to not risk drinking from any questionable water source, no matter how clean it looks or smells. Camping trips really go downhill when vomiting or diarrhea is involved. Either carry a water-sterilizing pen (very light) or boil water for ten minutes before using. Most public camping grounds have safe water supplies or even freshwater springs. Be sure to look for signs that indicate a water supply is not for drinking. Most parks will label their water sources if they are safe or not.

Out of all the camping tips, please remember this - water is more important than food in order to stay alive. Should the worst happens and you need to abandon your food to a hungry bear (for example), give up the food. The water is more important. If

G. A. Iron Cloud

you have a long walk from the fresh water source to your campsite and you happen to lose your canteen or water jug, use a non-lubricated condom to carry the water. It can hold over a gallon.

Chapter 11 Food

Things to consider

Though most people are passionate about camping in the summertime, it is something that the more intrepid also enjoy in the wintertime as well. Whatever season that you prefer to go camping, one thing is for sure and that is it's an adventure that few will want to pass up for there is always something that happens for which you were not prepared for.

I have camped in every season, and under just about every weather condition, so I know from personal experience that camping in the wintertime can be a miserable experience. Unless you have a lot of camping experience, leave the winter camping to the pros.

Duration of trip

You should make it a point to plan ahead regarding your camping food and these plans must include among other things the amount of time you plan on being out camping, because it is quite common for camping to cause your appetite to turn more voracious than when at home enjoying creature comforts. Thus, camping food is more than having enough quantity and should also take into account the nutritious value of the food, which should be your major consideration when choosing your camping food.

But, nutrition should not result in loss of wholesome and appetizing foods and it should also not take away any of the many pleasures that eating out in the outdoors involves. You must therefore also include energy bars that can come in handy every once in a while and have sufficient camping food to cook because there is certainly a lot of pleasure to be derived by cooking a meal over a campfire as well.

You also need to consider how to pack the camping food, which can tax your organizational skills, and it also means packing the meals separately.

Don't forget to mark the container so that you know what each packet contains rather than opening them to see what is inside. Also, you should pack the camping food in backpacks in an order in which you expect to consume the food and this forethought will pay handsome dividends when you are out hiking because it would mean that you don't have to unpack everything in order to access your packed food packets. Simplified: Pack the food you are going to eat last in the bottom of the pack and the food you are going to eat first at the very top.

In addition, you should also ensure that camping food does not mean that you need to forego cooking a traditional camp meal once each day which is an excellent way of enjoying the outdoors and which will add considerably to the pleasure of getting the most out of your camping experience.

Since high tech foodstuffs that are readily available, camping food has slowly begun to lose some of its charm, which is a pity because it has a special place in camping activities as it makes for some very pleasurable experiences and will provide memories that can be cherished for many years to come. So, don't go overboard with all those high tech foodstuffs -- give heavy consideration to the more conventional camping food as well. You will enjoy your camping much more.

G. A. Iron Cloud

Chapter 12 Dogs and Camping

Most camping guide omit an important participant in the camping experience - the family dog. A large number of campers take their children camping, and kids always want to include the family pooch as a camping member.

Your dog loves to be with the family and also loves to be outside. What a great treat for the family and dog to go camping together. Although you might think the dog is already packed with enough natural camping gear, indoor dogs need a little help adjusting to Mother Nature. Just like you need camping gear, so does your dog. Remember that each dog is different, so keep in mind the dog's special needs.

Doggy musts

In order to have a happy and safe camping trip, your dog must be healthy, up to date with his or her shots and worming pills. You'll run into lots of external parasites trying to hitch a ride on the dog, so be sure your dog is also up to date with any flea and tick treatment. If you are not sure if your dog can handle a camping trip, ask your vet. Remember, you will need to carry the dog's food, bedding and other camping gear that your dog can't. An arthritic

76

dog will hurt more in the cold and needs extra warmth. In the winter, when conditions are below freezing, think about shoes for your dog. Not only do they offer some insulation against the cold, they also protect paws from jagged edges of ice that may be on the ground.

Paw wear

There are a lot of surprises awaiting you and your dog on a camping trial - and some of them very uncomfortable to walk on. You can purchase camping gear for your dog that has been designed by dog musher's in Alaska. You can choose a paw wax or boots for extra comfort and protection for your dog's feet. They not only keep out any sharp objects like splinters and burrs, but they also keep ice from impacting in between your dog's toes. And they do help to keep the dog's paws clean when you both cuddle in the tent. You can find these in sporting goods shops and online camping supply stores.

Life vests

If you are going boating on your camping trip, don't forget a life vest for your dog. Not only will these insure your dog won't drown, but they are brightly colored enough for anyone to spot the dog should he or she get separated from you. Dogs are great swimmers, but often underestimate the surprisingly powerful currents of even six-inch deep streams. A bright vest will also warn any wildlife that a dog is approaching. For less than $50, they are a great investment.

Collapsible feeding bowls

When you're camping, you want everything to be as lightweight and flexible as possible for easy carrying and easier packing. There are many collapsible food and water dishes available wherever doggy products or camping gear are sold. They are popular items for walks, hikes, plus non-camping visits to Granny and for traveling.

Bring two Leashes - a long one and a short one

There will times when you don't want your dog running loose. Be sure to take a regular leash for your dog, and pack a long leash or a long rope with you. A short leash is handy for hiking when you don't want your dog running into the woods alone, and perhaps getting lost. A long rope or leash is necessary for when you have camp visitors or you simply don't want canine company during camp meals.

Tick and Flea Spray

Dogs are susceptible to woodland insects. Do your dog a favor and give it a spray now and then to protect it.

The Ultimate Camping Guide and Camping TIps

G. A. Iron Cloud

Chapter 13 Trailers

Owning or renting your camping trailer

Rather than roughing it when you next go camping there are other alternatives to seek out including renting or purchasing one of the many different models of camping trailers that are currently available on the market today. You can choose your camping trailer according to your needs and it could be anything from a hard-top tent trailer to an all-in one unit that is quite as good as a home on wheels.

Major factor is cost

Every type of camping trailer has its own advantages and disadvantages though the major factor that influences buyers of course its cost. Thus, you may opt for the camping trailer that is like a pop-up or fold down tent trailer which is quite inexpensive and ideally suited for the more common campgrounds and also where there is easy access by road.

The cheaper the camping trailer, the more likely it is that it will be made from aluminum or steel or even fiberglass and which has a steel bottom that has a lid which can be cranked up till it reaches a height of eight feet above your bed. Such camping trailers have a few bunks that can even are foldable, and which look a bit like tents though they are big enough to accommodate two grown-ups and in size they are as big as large double beds.

You will usually find that a common feature in all camping trailers is that of having permanent cupboards for storage where you can store your utensils as well as clothing and some supplies as well, while some models may even come with a fridge (small) and even sinks countertops as well as cooking surfaces. And, in the middle you could even have a table that can be collapsed when not in use, and which even has bench like seating arrangement.

Some of the more modern camping trailers even have electricity wiring in them, and once hooked to a generator, can become as comfortable as a moving home.

However, before you choose your camping trailer, you need to exercise care and must consider your budget as too spending requirements. You should also look for durability so that your investment lasts you many years and when taken care of well and maintained properly should give you long lasting service.

Thus, you would be well advised to spend your time researching various options and even considering renting out a camping trailer if you don't want to own one, or do not plan extensive camping trips.

A home away from home

There are a lot of camping trailers available in the market today. The designs vary from conventional to luxurious. Many manufacturers of camping trailers can custom design a trailer with every conceivable amenity that can be added to camping trailers at the request of the person ordering it.

Since camping trailers are to be an extension of a person's home, there is a need to make it comfortable and easy to manage. There are many different kinds of camping trailers and these include recreational vehicles, teardrop trailers, folding campers and many more.

Different camping trailers

The RV or recreational vehicle is actually more of a motor home than a trailer since in most designs of the RV, it is one whole vehicle instead of a vehicle with a trailer attached. These kinds of camping trailers is where the drivers' seat can be seen by anybody else in the trailer unlike where the trailer is being towed, it is just an extension of the vehicle towing it.

There are two classes of RVs. A lot of people don't know the difference between a Class A and a Class C RV.

There are many factors that you should consider if you're thinking or buying a recreational vehicle. There are three main different classes which have different attributes depending on your preference. Class A RV's are becoming less popular as they are very expensive to run, especially with the rise of fuel prices.

Picking the right RV can be a very challenging job if you don't know what you're looking for.

Below is a list of the advantages and disadvantages of each type of RV so you can get a better understanding if you're new to the motor home industry.

Class A

These are motorized bus style vehicles so the main attraction is the fact they are very practical. People that travel a lot of plan on taking many family vacations should consider one of these.

One of the big pitfalls with Class A motorhomes is the initial cost and running costs. They consume large amounts of fuel so they can be costly in the long run.

The larger Class A motorhomes can be hard to manoeuvre which tends to put many people off.

Class B

Class B recreational vehicles are one of the most popular RV's in today's world as they are very economical and easily drivable. You can practically take them anywhere which appeals to many people as they are not restricted as they are not too big.

The downside to this specific type of motor home is that they are small, you can only fit a limited amount of people inside comfortably and they have minimum storage space.

Class C

A Class C RV looks like a large camper shell built on a large pickup bed. The main characteristic that stands out on a Class C is the safety. They are very secure and economical to drive. They make great family vehicles as you can regularly go on family vacations bringing you closer then before.

You are restricted in areas you can take this type of RV as they can become overweight if you have excess luggage or if it's too long.

A good resource for comparing RV's is the RV Comparison Guide which can be found online at JR Consumer Resources. They are a consumer based company that rates RV manufacturers and compares each manufacturer regarding customer satisfaction, quality of construction and resale value.

Teardrop trailers are camping trailers that are rather small and ideal for just one to two people to use. It is hitched to a vehicle and towed to the area where you wish to camp. These are usually used during hunting trips and other short single person stays in camp. It is called a teardrop trailer because of its shape.

A folding trailer is a trailer that is also towed by any vehicle. These types of camping trailers have sides that can be folded or collapsed to facilitate better storage or towing. It is basically small and cannot be slept in. It is more or less used for storage or things which one needs for camping. Travel trailers are camping trailers that are towed by a vehicle and have rigid sides. It usually has a frame hitch or a bumper hitch, which is used to attach to the vehicle used to tow it.

Other kinds of camping trailers are the fifth wheel trailer and the park model. The fifth wheel trailers are different because of the way it is attached to the vehicle towing it. The trailer head is extended to be able to reach the top of the vehicle that is towing it. It is attached to the vehicle with the use of a fifth wheel coupling hence the name, fifth wheel trailer. The park model trailer is a trailer that is not designed for "dry camping". It is pretty much the same other trailers except for this feature.

Chapter 14 Survival

Camping Equipment is also your survival kit

In the event of a major disaster, your camping equipment can be your lifeline for survival. Don't discount the usefulness of tents, sleeping bags, water purifiers or any other camping equipment. Many people buy camping stuff - whether new or discount camping equipment - and simply stash them in a garage or attic for 51 weeks of the year. This is a waste of good stuff.

Water purifiers

There are many portable water purifiers that can be found in boating, sporting goods or camping supplies shops. Don't discount camping equipment such as this. You never know when your home water supply might be polluted or contaminated. If you can't boil your water before using it (say, if the stove is out, too), then you can use one of the many portable water purifiers. Water purifiers can be tablets (which make the water taste like pool water, but it'll be safe), filter jugs or ultra violet pens. The ultra violet pens are the newest and coolest of water purifiers. It was originally designed for camping, but can be used in any emergency situation - or any situation where you want to show off your latest techie toy.

Chapter 15 Receipes

Rather than including a lot of recipes in this book, I recommend you definitely purchase a recipe book that is devoted to camping recipes. It's fun to experiment with recipes that are designed for a campfire. You can find almost any type of recipe book you want on Amazon. Just search on "Camping recipes" and you'll find a selection of several hundred books to chose from.

For obvious reasons, I recommend buying a large paperback book, rather than a digital book. You'll find that a large paperback recipe book is a lot easier to read by the light of a campfire than a small recipe book with small print.

Simple Food Ideas for Camping:

1) Any packaged dinner mix from the grocery and packed in ziploc baggies ie, Macaroni & Cheese, Rice-a-Roni, Broccoli and Cheese, etc. There are tons of these things available today. If they call for milk, then carry powdered milk in baggies.

G. A. Iron Cloud

2) Instant oatmeal and instant grits and bagels are great for breakfast. Again, powdered milk can be used with these. Get some of the new Fantastic Foods hot cereal mixes--they are warm and filling.

3) Dehydrated vegetables and full meals can be found in camping stores. Add dried peas to a box of mac & cheese, for instance

4) Try Ramen noodle soups, or any of those "soup in a cup"s (that can be packaged in baggies so they take up less room).

5) Dehydrated bean flakes that mix up almost instantly with water are available in HFS. Mix these with some cooked minute rice and put in a tortilla. Yum! Flavor them with onion, garlic, cumin powders.

6) Cheesepacks . Again, the fat may not be so bad if you are hiking all day. And if it's cold, then the fat is almost necessary to help stay warm. (You need a lot more calories when it's cold. Add a hunk to any soup, pasta, rice, or dehydrated veggies you're cooking.

7) Pasta, pasta, pasta. Top it with sauces made from the dry package mixes. A lot of these are tasty. High in sodium and preservatives sometimes, but for a couple of meals they won't hurt you.

8) Instant mashed potatoes that can be mixed with the powdered milk or water only. Make up an instant gravy to go top.

9) Dried fruit can be cooked in some water and put on top of a piece of angel food cake for dessert. Add some cinnamon and Tang (in lieu of orange juice) and you approximate a Cooking Light recipe.

10) Dry veggie burger mixes make a great meal. Most of them make up with water only and many are quite tasty.

How to Make a Box Oven

Box ovens are handy for camping and are easiyl constructed at the camp grounds. It's also fun to cook on an oven that you've contructed yourself. It's also a great family project and fun for the kids. Total construction time is only about 15 minutes.

Materials:
1 Brick (or flat rock)
1 pk Aluminum foil, heavy-duty
1 Corrugated cardboard box
1 Metal pie pan,old
3 Coat hangers
4 Charcoal briquets,lit

1. Cover the inside and outside of the box completely with 3 or 4 layers of aluminum foil,

including the flaps. Lay box on level ground so that the flaps open oven-style (front-door   style is OK, too).

2. Straighten the coat hangers, then run them through the sides of the box about 2/3 of the way up from the bottom to form a rack.

3. Set brick in bottom. Place live coals into pie pan/pie plate. Put pan on brick (don't forget, the PIE PAN IS HOT! Use an oven mitt or hot pad).

4. Place food to be cooked onto coat-hanger rack and close oven door.

Watch carefully, checking often. Each live coal increases the temperature by about 80 degrees Fahrenheit.

Receipes
It's best that you purchase a camping receipe book. I suggest that you get a paperback instead of a Kindle book.   But here's a few receipes that are easy and fun to make.

Grilled Cheeze
Sandwiches can be made without a pan--use a buddy burner if you have one or wrap the prepared sandwich in foil and place just above the coals (cooks real fast). To make it a more complete meal add tomatoes, onions and cold cuts or any combination of your choice before cooking.

Kebobs

Easy to make and requires no pans. If using wooden skewers, soak them in water to slow down the burning and make sure you can cook without holding by hand over the fire; if using metal ones make sure each person has a good glove to hold it with or there is a proper handle on it.

Make kebobs with wieners, smokies, sausage or meatballs. Pre cook chicken, turkey, ham or any other meat cubes. Use a variety of veggies such as peppers, canned taters, tomatoes, mushrooms, etc. As it is cooking, brush with BBQ sauce or teriyaki sauce if so desired.

Rice Cooked in a sleeping bag.

Take instant rice in 2 heavy duty zip lock bags. Add slightly less than normal amount of boiling water, (it must be at a full boil), add some raisins, nuts or some cinnamon and sugar,
or whatever other flavoring you desire. Zip it up tight and place in a sleeping bag (insulation). The rice will cook in about 20 minutes. Once the rice is done, you can add cinnamon, nutmeg, raisins and nuts to make it a dessert or snack; or you can use it as a side dish by adding butter, soy sauce or canned gravy.

Bread

Add grated cheddar or parmesan cheese to butter, spread on bread slices (french or Italian loaves sliced thick work best) wrap in foil and put on coals or on a grate above the coals.

Hot Dogs

Wrap hot dogs in biscuit wraps and cook them on a stick or wrap very loosely in foil and place on grate above fire for 15 to 30 minutes (time will depend on the heat of the fire and the weather. To make these more fun add cheese, onions, mustard, ketchup, pickles, bacon bits, etc. before wrapping.
If using a stick, only add a little bit or the wrap will rip.

Potato Dinner

Take a raw potato. Hollow out the center of a raw potato leaving about 1/2 inch all the way around with skin attached. Fill the center with spiced hamburger with a bit of tomato sauce or sausage pieces. Wrap tightly in foil and place on coals. Serve with cheese or garlic bread and a salad or some steamed or canned veggies. To steam veggies, slice thinly and make a foil pack and add a little water; seal and place on or over hot coals. Check after a 1/2 hour. Potato will take about an hour.

Onio Skin Hamburger

Cut a large onion in half cross-wise and remove most of the center, leaving about 3 or 4 layers. Mix up a hamburger mixture of your favorite seasonings and press into the hollowed out onion skin. Place directly on the coals for about 20 to 25 minutes.

Bacon and Eggs (try this it's fun)

Using a paper lunch bag, place 2 pieces of bacon in bottom of bag. Crack 1 egg on top, roll down bag tightly; poke stick through bag and hold over fire. Bag will not burn. It will take about 5 minutes to have bacon and eggs. DO NOT ADD EXTRA BACON AS THE GREASE WILL CAUSE THE BOTTOM TO FALL OUT OF THE BAG. At the same time make toast by sticking a piece of bread on the end of stick, turn as necessary.

Bag Omelet

Use a good quality ziplock type bag. Break 1 to 3 eggs into the bag, add a tablespoon of milk per egg, add cheese, bacon bits, peppers, onions, mushrooms or whatever you like in an
omelette to the bag. Close the bag tightly, much all together and drop bag into boiling water (water should be at a full boil. It will take 3 to 8 minutes depending on how many bags are in the water. Can be thrown back into the water if you find yours isn't done enough.

Boiled Egg

Place egg in a paper cup used for hot coffee (a paper one without the wax coating). Cover the egg with water and sit the cup on the coals. Have the seam on the cup away from the flames as the cup may split open on the seam. Bring the water to a boil and boil for 10 minutes adding more water as necessary to keep the egg covered. The cup will not catch fire as long as you make sure that there is enough water in the cup.

Orange Skin Biscuit and Eggs
Cut an orange in half cross-wise and scoop out the insides and eat. Break an egg into the hollow rind and set directly onto the coals and cook for 10 to 15 minutes, or until the center is
done. For biscuits, mix Bisquick as directed and fill rind 3/4's full and cook as above until toothpick comes out clean (no doughy goo on it).

Orange Skin Cake
Have each person eat an orange by cutting a thin slice from the top and eating the pulp with a spoon leaving the skin in tact. (They could have the orange for breakfast and save the shells in a zip lock.) Mix a white or spice cake mix as directed on box. Pour mix into rind until 3/4's full, put the thin slice on the top and wrap in foil, place on coals and cook for 10 to 15 minutes.

Baked Apples
Cut the apples in quarters, remove seeds and place on shiny side of a sheet of foil. Sprinkle with brown sugar, cinnamon, raisins and dot with butter. Wrap tightly and place on coals for 10 to 15 minutes.

Bread on a stick

Use a stick about the width of a broom handle. Cover about 1 1/2 feet with foil, shiny side out. Grease the foil well, wrap canned crescent rolls around it and bake over the hot coals. Can also use biscuit mix. After mixing biscuits make a tope of the dough and wrap around stick leaving a little space between wraps. Serve with jam or honey.

Pudding in a bag

Using a good ziplock bag, divide instant pudding into portions in the bags, add the right amount of milk, close the bag and mush with fingers. In about 5 minutes you'll have pudding. Eat it right from the bag.

Here's a few more recipes.

Camp Potatoes

4 Potatoes,sliced
4 Onions,sliced
4 T Butter or margarine
10 oz Cheddar cheese,sharp
Salt & pepper to taste

Grease a large square of heavy foil. Arrange sliced potatoes on foil, sprinkle with salt and pepper and cover with sliced onions. Add chunks of butter or margarine. Wrap and seal foil. Cook over hot coals on a grill until done (30 or 40 minutes depending on fire). Open foil and add thin-sliced cheddar strips.

Cover again and grill for a couple of minutes, until cheddar melts.

Camp Baked Potatoes
6 Baking potatoes
1/4 t Garlic powder
1 Onion,chopped
1/2 t Lemon pepper
4 oz Green chiles
Aluminum foil
4 oz Black olives,chopped

1. Scrub and chop baking potatoes into pieces, but do not peel.
2. Prepare 6-8 square pieces of heavy-duty aluminum foil, one piece per serving. Place equal portions of the chopped potatoes and other ingredients on each foil square. Fold the foil burrito style and twist the ends.
3. Place on campfire grill for about 45-55 minutes. If you can safely take along margarine, you might want to add a teaspoon or so to each packet before grilling.

Hobo Pie
1 lb Ground beef
4 Carrots sliced
2 Potatoes cubed
1 md Onion,sliced in 1/4" pieces
Butter

Form hamburger patties and put one patty,with individual of whole carrots,sliced potatoes and sliced onions,on a sheet of aluminum foil. Brush everything with butter and sprinkle with salt and pepper.
Fold foil over food and place on charcoal or open fire.
Cook for an hour,turning every 15 minutes. Chicken can be substituted for the hamburger meat.

Here are a few things to think about.

Water, Water, Water

You can skimp on ingredients or even food in all easy camping recipes, but you cannot skimp on water. You will need several liters a day in order to have the energy to keep going (depending on the weather). If you forget all of the other easy camping recipes presented here, please remember to make getting at least two liters of water a day as your top priority. You can survive about three months without food. You can only survive three days without water.

Peanut Butter

The easiest of easy camping recipes is to pack a plastic jar of peanut butter. Bread, crackers or biscuits are optional. You can also pack your peanut butter in a plastic baggie to save on space. Just make sure you buy a baggie with a good seal, like the ones with plastic slides. You definitely don't need peanut butter smeared on everything in your backpack.

You will be using a lot of calories, so you need calorie-laden food. Peanut butter, in one sense, is much better for you than energy bars because energy bars cause you to drink a lot of water with them. If you are camping where fresh water is plentiful, then go for the energy or daily nutrition bars. But if you are not sure, pack peanut butter and chocolate.

Meals in a pouch

Because weight may be an issue, one of the easiest camping recipes is to pack dehydrated or fully hydrated meals that come in pouches. These are called MREs, or Meals Ready to Eat. The hydrated ones do not need the addition of any water - they are basically canned meals stored in pouches rather than in heavy cans. These pack a lot of calories and are quite tasty. In worse case scenarios, they are perfectly safe to be eaten cold straight from the pouch.

Buying your food

If you are willing to put in the miles, don't forget you can always walk to and from a nearby store, café or snack bar every day for your meals. It certainly is one of the easiest ways to have food on your trip (although it is the least fun), and you might even get hot food or a hot drink, too. The only drawback is that you have to walk to your food source every day, rain or shine, and pay in legal tender.

Make sure stores are nearby before you rely on them for meals. Google the area using Google maps to see what is nearby and how far away they are from your camping site. Google Earth is also a handy resource. As extra insurance, call them to make sure they are still in business. Many small stores and restaurants open and close under different owners, and sometimes close down permanently.

Chapter 16 Resources

Here are 20 plus of my favorite online camping resources:

1.) KOA campgrounds are available in 44 different states nationwide, which makes them a great choice for almost any destination. The campgrounds are often located near popular attractions, busy interstates, or natural wonders, and are easily accessible. This site contains national parks, state parks, directories, camping tips, various camping associations, and blogs. http://www.allcampgrounds.com/articles/tips/choosing-a-koa-campground.html

2.) The America's Great Outdoors (AGO) Initiative is developing a 21st Century conservation and recreation agenda to help ensure lasting conservation solutions rising from the American people - the premise is the protection of our natural heritage is a non-partisan objective shared by all Americans. http://www.americasgreatoutdoors.gov/

3.) The "Top 100 Family Campgrounds" were selected based on criteria requested by family campers including park amenities, beautiful outdoor scenery, and educational facilities.
http://www.thecampingclub.com/zztop100/top100list.html

4.) National Volcano Early Warning System.
http://pubs.usgs.gov/of/2005/1164/

5.) Published by the Smithsonian Institution Press - For those who like to venture off the beaten path, this book is a must-have. It's filled with the best-kept secrets about 175 unique public land sites throughout the West, with several eastern sites included for good measure ... take a peek.
http://www.blm.gov/wo/st/en/res/Education_in_BLM/Learning_Landscapes.html

6.) The compilation and dissemination of current information on bird distribution. Checklists developed that indicate the seasonal occurrence of birds in state, federal, and private management areas, nature preserves, and other areas of special interest in the United States.
http://www.npwrc.usgs.gov/resource/birds/chekbird/index.htm

7.) Offers a free directory of campgrounds (camps, rv parks) in California, USA. All camping listings come with direct contacts, addresses, telephones,

maps, GPS waypoints, photos and even weather charts.
http://www.ca-camping-review.com/

8.) A Camping and Campgrounds Resource for over 13,000 campgrounds - including State parks, national parks, RV Parks, RV camping, and local campgrounds.
http://www.camping-usa.com/

9.) Find the best campgrounds has over 16,000 campgrounds listed nationwide with information on the amenities, location, and camp details. Just type in the location box your destination of interest and select a search radius to view a campground.
http://www.campgrounds.findthebest.com/

10.) Recreational enthusiasts can search this national database of nearly 2 million physical and cultural geographic features in the United States.
http://geonames.usgs.gov/

11.) Go Camping America makes it easy to find your next camping adventure. Use the map to search state-by-state or search by city.
http://www.gocampingamerica.com/findPark.aspx

12.) Ever wonder what an aerial view of your camping area might look like? Terraserver is one of the world's largest online databases, providing free public access to a vast collection of maps and aerial photographs of the United States.

http://terraserver-usa.com/

13.) Complete range of traditional maps and features enabling you to create your own map to explore the great outdoors and locate access points for your camping destinations.
http://nationalatlas.gov/index.html

14.) Recreational enthusiasts can view their local weather forecasts. The site includes weather watches, weather hazards, warnings, statements and advisories for the nation
http://www.srh.noaa.gov/

15.) The Recreation One-Stop initiative is intended to enhance customer satisfaction with recreational experiences on public lands. It will improve access to recreation-related information generated by the Federal government, streamline the systems used to manage that information, and increase the sharing of recreation-related information among government and non-government organizations.
http://www.recreation.gov/recFacilityActivitiesHome
Action.do?goto=camping.htm

16.) The NRRS has formed a partnership between the U.S. Army Corps of Engineers, National Park Service, Bureau of Land Management, the Bureau of Land Management and the USDA Forest Service. Reservations may also be made by calling toll free, 1-877-444-6777. Reserve campsites, cabins, day use, and wilderness permits.

http://www.recreation.gov/

17.) Pick the State of your choice for ideal camping and recreation facilities
http://recreation.usgs.gov/state_parks.html

18.) This site details all the information you need to take a look at, before you explore that hiking adventure.
http://www.thehikinglife.com/skills/choosing-a-campsite/

19.) This Google based site lists over 15,400 public campgrounds in the Lower 48 United States, includes a search/locate/compare function and a downloadable POI list.
http://www.ultimatecampgrounds.com/

20.) This site offers listings of activities, videos, guides blogs and information for camp people ... by camp people.
http://www.ultimatecampresource.com/

21.) Virginia is for Lovers - listing of camping sites and RVing in Virginia
http://www.virginia.org/CampingRVing/

22.) Hiking and Camping Search Engine
http://www.webdirectory.com/Parks_and_Recreation/Hiking_and_Camping/

About the Author

G.A. Iron Cloud was raised in the great wilderness of Montana. He is an avid camper and fisherman.

He is dedicated to preserving America's nature and wilderness.